EATING RIGHT WITH MYPLATE

Fruit Group

by Megan Borgert-Spaniol

BELLWETHER MEDIA • MINNEAPOLIS, MN

Note to Librarians, Teachers, and Parents:

Blastoff! Readers are carefully developed by literacy experts and combine standards-based content with developmentally appropriate text.

Level 1 provides the most support through repetition of high-frequency words, light text, predictable sentence patterns, and strong visual support.

Level 2 offers early readers a bit more challenge through varied simple sentences, increased text load, and less repetition of high-frequency words.

Level 3 advances early-fluent readers toward fluency through increased text and concept load, less reliance on visuals, longer sentences, and more literary language.

Level 4 builds reading stamina by providing more text per page, increased use of punctuation, greater variation in sentence patterns, and increasingly challenging vocabulary.

Level 5 encourages children to move from "learning to read" to "reading to learn" by providing even more text, varied writing styles, and less familiar topics.

Whichever book is right for your reader, Blastoff! Readers are the perfect books to build confidence and encourage a love of reading that will last a lifetime!

Reader

This edition first published in 2012 by Bellwether Media, Inc.

No part of this publication may be reproduced in whole or in part without written permission of the publisher. For information regarding permission, write to Bellwether Media, Inc., Attention: Permissions Department, 5357 Penn Avenue South, Minneapolis, MN 55419.

Library of Congress Cataloging-in-Publication Data

Borgert-Spaniol, Megan, 1989-
 Fruit group / by Megan Borgert-Spaniol.
   p. cm. – (Blastoff! readers. Eating right with myplate)
 Summary: "Relevant images match informative text in this introduction to the fruit group. Intended for students in kindergarten through third grade"– Provided by publisher.
 Includes bibliographical references and index.
 ISBN 978-1-60014-755-5 (hardcover : alk. paper)
 1. Fruit in human nutrition–Juvenile literature. 2. Fruit–Juvenile literature. I. Title.
 QP144.F78B67 2012
 613.2–dc23   2011033122

Printed in the United States of America, North Mankato, MN.

010112   1207

Contents

The Fruit Group

Fruits are **naturally** sweet and low in **fat**.

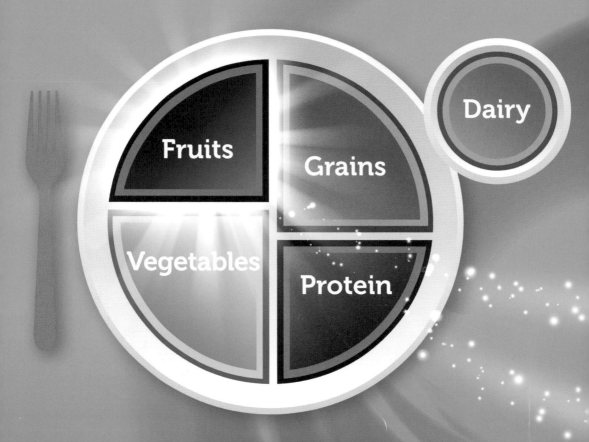

The red part of **MyPlate** is the Fruit Group.

1 serving = 1 small apple
            1 small watermelon wedge
            1 large banana
            32 grapes
            1 large orange
            8 large strawberries

Why Are Fruits Good For You?

Citrus fruit

are full o

...amin C keeps your **gums**
...eeth healthy. It also
...your body heal...

Bananas and orange juice are rich in **potassium**.

... can keep your muscles strong. It gives you energy to play.

Raspberries, kiwis, and pears are loaded with **fiber.**

12

Choosing Fruits

Fruits can be dried, canned, frozen, or fresh.

Choose canned fruit that comes in 100% fruit juice or water.

15

Eating Fruits

Fruits can add sweetness to any meal. Top your breakfast cereal with berries.

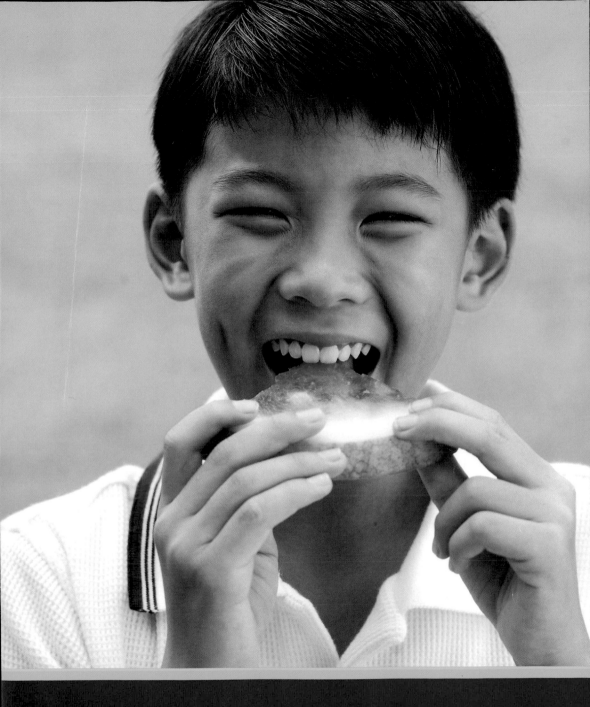

...ve a slice of watermelon
...nch. Try raisins or dried
...or a snack.

17

Make a fruit salad with kiwi, berries, apples, and pears.

Blending milk and ice to make a smoothie. Frozen fruit bars are another cold treat.

Find fresh ways to enjoy fruits every day.

...ey are ripe with health

...efits and full of flavor!

Glossary

citrus fruits—fruits that are often peeled and squeezed for their juice; oranges, lemons, limes, and grapefruit are examples of citrus fruits.

fat—a part of some foods that gives you energy and helps your body use vitamins; too much of certain fats is bad for your heart.

fiber—the part of a plant that stays whole as it moves through your body

gums—the soft, pink tissues that hold your teeth in place

MyPlate—a guide that shows the kinds and amounts of food you should eat each day

naturally—the way that something is in nature; fruits are naturally sweet.

potassium—a part of some foods that keeps your muscles healthy and gives you energy

smoothie—a cold drink made by blending ice, milk, and fruit

vitamin C—a part of some foods that helps keep your teeth and gums healthy; vitamin C also helps your body heal.

To Learn More

AT THE LIBRARY

Ehlert, Lois. *Eating the Alphabet: Fruits & Vegetables from A to Z*. San Diego, Calif.: Harcourt, 2006.

French, Vivian. *Oliver's Fruit Salad*. New York, N.Y.: Orchard Books, 1998.

Richards, Jean. *A Fruit is a Suitcase for Seeds*. Brookfield, Conn.: Millbrook Press, 2002.

ON THE WEB

Learning more about the Fruit Group is as easy as 1, 2, 3.

1. Go to www.factsurfer.com.

2. Enter "Fruit Group" into the search box.

3. Click the "Surf" button and you will see a list of related Web sites.

With factsurfer.com, finding more information is just a click away.

Index

The images in this book are reproduced through the courtesy of: Juan Martinez, front cover, pp. 7, 8, 10, 12; Kzenon, p. 4; Viktor, p. 5; U.S. Department of Agriculture, Center for Nutrition Policy and Promotion, p. 6; Andrew Olney / Getty Images, p. 9; Jupiterimages / Getty Images, p. 11; Masterfile, p. 13; Elena Schweitzer, p. 14; Zhukov Oleg, p. 15; Sven Schermer, p. 16; Asia Images / Masterfile, p. 17; shebeko, p. 18; Juice Images / Photolibrary, p. 19; Judith Haeusler / Getting Images, pp. 20-21.